Talented Animals

Written by Keith Pigdon

Series Consultant: Linda Hoyt

WorldWise™
Content-based Learning

Contents

Chapter 1:

Staying alive 4

Case study:
An elephant's trunk 6

Chapter 2:

Masters of movement 8

Masters on land 8

Masters in the air 12

Masters in the water 14

Chapter 3:
Extraordinary senses 16

Seeing the world 17

Detecting sound 18

Taste and smell 20

Hidden senses 21

Chapter 4:
Special body parts 22

Long fingers 24

Long tongues 25

Birds and their beaks 26

Chapter 5:
Using tools 28

Using sticks as tools 28

Using stones and rocks as tools 30

Glossary 31

Index 32

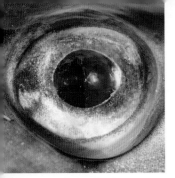

Chapter 1:

Staying alive

Animals come in many different shapes and sizes, and they look very different from each other. But have you ever wondered why some animals have huge ears or eyes or noses, or why some have hard beaks? How an animal looks and how it behaves help it to stay alive.

So what does an animal need to stay alive? It needs food and water, it needs to protect itself from danger and it needs to reproduce to make sure that its **species** survives.

Some can run, swim or fly extremely fast. Others have enhanced **senses**, such as incredibly good eyesight or super-sensitive hearing. Some have especially **adapted** body parts like beaks or trunks or very long tongues to help them survive. And others use tools such as sticks and stones.

Walruses

Chameleon

What helps each of these animals to stay alive?

Hare

Kingfisher

Case study: An elephant's trunk

Elephants are the largest animals that live on land. The trunk of an elephant is its best-known feature. An elephant's trunk is an extension of its upper lip and nose.

There are many ways an elephant uses its trunk to help it survive every day.

Feeding

An elephant can eat up to 300 kilograms of food a day. It uses its trunk to grasp and pull up grasses and other plants, as well as pulling down leaves from a tree. Its trunk can reach up to six metres into a tree. The tip of the trunk is so sensitive that tiny things like nuts can be grasped and put in the mouth.

Lifting

An elephant can lift heavy objects such as trees and logs with its trunk.

Smelling

An elephant can smell things nearly four kilometres away.

Drinking

An elephant drinks up to 190 litres of water a day. Its trunk can hold about 7.5 litres of water. The elephant sucks the water into its trunk and squirts it into its mouth.

Trunk facts
- An elephant's trunk grows to 1.8 metres long.
- It can weigh up to 130 kilograms.
- A trunk has thousands of muscles (some say 40,000), but no bones.

Communicating

An elephant uses its trunk to greet other elephants and to communicate with them. It can make loud trumpeting noises as well as low-pitched noises.

Grooming

Elephants use their trunks to squirt water and throw dust over themselves to keep cool.

Defence

Elephants use their trunks as weapons.

Touching

The tip of an elephant's trunk is very sensitive and is used to gently touch other elephants.

Chapter 2:

Masters of movement

All animals can move about in the place where they live, but some can move extremely fast to catch food and to survive. They can run or jump great distances, swing through trees, swim through water and fly through the air.

Masters on land

Many animals move around on land by walking, running or jumping. Some can reach great speeds or leap great distances.

How fast can they run?	
Animal	kilometres per hour
Cheetah	100
Pronghorn antelope	90
Racehorse	70
Kangaroo	65
Emu	48
Human	37
Elephant	30
Black mamba (snake)	19
House spider	2
Sloth	0.2

Cheetah

Master runners

Cheetahs can run faster than any other animal on Earth. They can reach speeds of 100 kilometres per hour over short distances. A cheetah's backbone can bend a long way. This allows it to bring its hind legs well forward to take a very long stride.

Cheetahs hunt other animals to eat. They twist and turn as they chase their prey. The table on page 8 shows how fast cheetahs are compared with other animals.

Did you know?

A cheetah uses a great deal of energy when running fast, so it can't keep going at top speed for a long time.

Master climbers and swingers

Animals that live in trees move easily among the branches. Monkeys use their strong hands to cling to trees. Some monkeys and ring-tailed possums can use their tails to grip branches, leaving their hands free to find food.

Gibbons

Find out more

Gibbons are one of the most athletic animals in the trees. They use their long arms to swing themselves through the treetops. Their long fingers and toes are used like hooks for swinging from tree to tree.

Kangaroos

Master jumpers

Some fast-moving mammals have developed strong back legs. Kangaroos use their powerful **hind limbs** to bound across open areas. They can leap along at speeds of up to 62 kilometres per hour. Other animals of a similar size use more energy than a kangaroo when they travel at the same speed.

How far can they jump?	
Animal	Distance (metres)
Red kangaroo	12.1
Mountain lion	12.1
Human	8.8
Jackrabbit	7.6
Frog	5.5
Flea	0.3

Think about ...

Monkeys are not the only animals that are great at jumping from tree to tree. Can you think of other animals that glide among the treetops?

11

Masters in the air

Birds are the fastest flying animals.

Golden eagles are the fastest members of the eagle family. They are powerful and majestic fliers that glide effortlessly on air currents. Golden eagles are also incredible acrobats. They can dive straight down with their bodies spinning to catch prey.

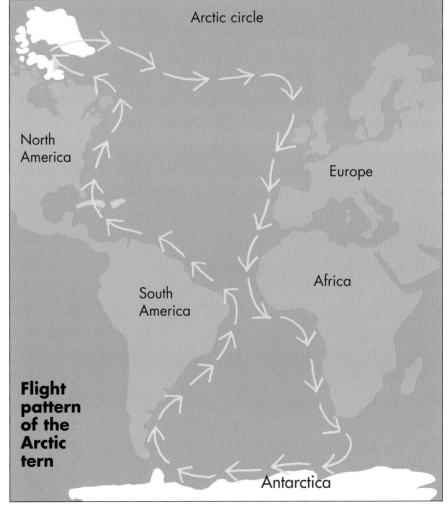

Flight pattern of the Arctic tern

Golden eagle

How fast can they fly?	
Animal	**kilometres per hour**
Peregrine falcon	200
Spine-tailed swift	170
Golden eagle	130
Canada goose	100
Great horned owl	60
Dragonfly	56
Bat	25
Bee	15

Some birds fly incredibly long distances to reach breeding grounds or to escape freezing cold weather. The Arctic tern makes the longest migratory flight of any bird. It flies from the Arctic circle in the north, to the Antarctic ice pack in the south, and back again in one year. This means it flies about 35,000 kilometres in a year, which is about the same as a trip right around the world.

Arctic terns live in colonies of hundreds of birds. It is very noisy until the moment the birds are about to migrate. Then the whole colony goes silent and the birds all fly away together.

Arctic tern

Did you know?

Arctic terns see the most daylight of any animal, because they are in the Arctic in the northern summer, and the Antarctic in the southern summer. Both of these places have more than 20 hours of daylight during summer.

Find out more

Bony fish have a **swim bladder** that saves their energy. Find out how this swim bladder works and how it helps bony fish.

Masters in the water

Animals that live in water such as fish, whales and dolphins have to be excellent swimmers.

Fish have bodies that are different shapes and sizes, but all are well suited to swimming. They use their fins or flippers and their tails to move forward and to steer.

The sailfish is the fastest swimming fish. It can reach speeds up to 100 kilometres per hour. Sailfish have a large fin on the top of their long bodies. Powerful muscles push them through the water at great speeds.

Sailfish

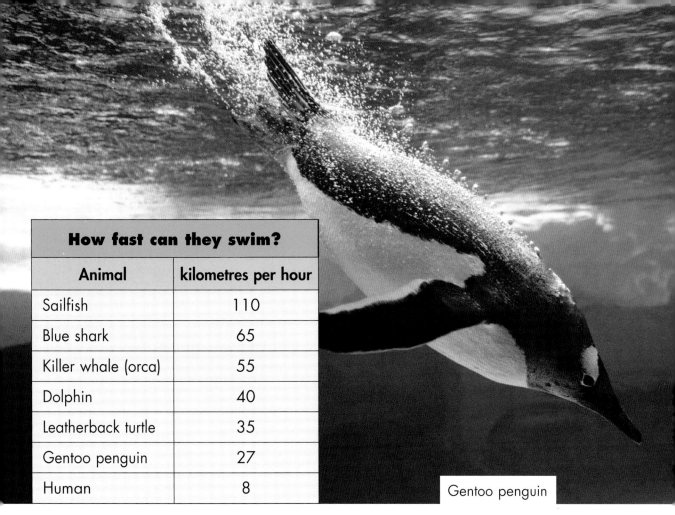

How fast can they swim?	
Animal	kilometres per hour
Sailfish	110
Blue shark	65
Killer whale (orca)	55
Dolphin	40
Leatherback turtle	35
Gentoo penguin	27
Human	8

Gentoo penguin

Many land-dwelling animals are also able to move through water to get their food. Platypuses, beavers and otters spend most of their lives in water. They have webbed feet to help them swim.

Many seabirds are excellent swimmers and divers. Some, such as the wandering albatross, spend most of their lives at sea catching fish, squid and other sea animals. Seabirds have feathers that are waterproof and webbed feet to help them swim.

Penguins can swim underwater to catch fish to eat. They use their wings like flippers and their feet and tails to help them steer.

Find out more

The emperor penguin can dive to 270 metres and stay underwater for 20 minutes. Are there any other birds that can do this?

Chapter 3:

Extraordinary senses

Most animals have the same **senses** as humans: they can see, hear, taste, smell and feel. Some animals, however, have senses that are much better developed than the human senses. And some animals have senses that humans don't have, such as **echolocation** and **heat sensors**.

Animals use their senses to help them find food, to sense danger and to reproduce. Their senses help them to stay alive.

Find out more

Birds of prey have very large eyes. Why do birds of prey have such large eyes?

How much further than humans can they see?

Bald eagle

Chameleon

Seeing the world

Birds of prey and diving seabirds can see much better than other animals. This helps them to find food at a distance.

Long-eared owl

A bird's-eye view

- Falcons can see small objects that are 1.6 kilometres away.
- Vultures can see prey from a height of 4,000 kilometres.
- Hawks can see four times further than humans. They can see from six metres what most people can only see from 1.5 metres.
- Golden eagles can spot a rabbit from over 1.6 kilometres away.
- Owls can turn their heads three quarters of the way around (270 degrees). In order to move their heads so far they have 14 **vertebrae** that are loosely connected to make their necks more flexible.
  Humans have only seven vertebrae in their necks.
- The eyes of birds of prey have three eyelids that give them extra protection. The third one is partially see-through. This allows the bird to protect its eyes while still being able to see when attacking prey.

Fennec fox

Detecting sound

Some animals use sound to locate prey, to signal and give warnings, to show fear and to find a mate. These animals depend on sound for their survival.

The fennec fox lives in the desert in northern Africa. It has very large ears that help it to pick up very faint sounds. These foxes can turn their ears to hear sounds from all directions. The fennec fox can hear large insects walking over sand.

Humpback whale

Whales are experts at communicating. Each whale of the same **species** has its own songs that it repeats at intervals to communicate with other members of the species. These songs are different in different oceans and change over the years. Other whales can hear these songs from great distances. Scientists are not exactly sure why whales sing to each other, but they think that whales use songs as part of their **mating ritual**.

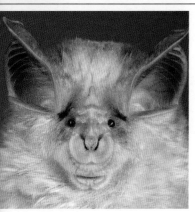

Bats can sense their prey up to six metres away by using echolocation.

Echolocation

Some animals such as bats and dolphins use sounds in a very specific way to find food. They can make short high-pitched squeaks or beeps. When these sounds hit an object they bounce back to the animal like an echo. This is called echolocation. From the echoes, these animals know the object's size, location and how it is moving.

Dolphins

Dolphins have very good eyesight, but in murky waters it is hard to see, so dolphins use sound to locate objects such as food. Sound travels through water more easily than light does, making it easier to hear than to see.

Dolphins make these sounds in the area just below the blowhole. They use the sound information to form a picture of their surroundings.

19

Taste and smell

Many animals use smell and taste to find food and to check whether it is safe to eat. They also use smell and taste to recognise prey, mates, family and enemies, and to sense danger.

The polar bear has a very good sense of smell. It can smell a dead animal from 20 kilometres away. Polar bears can also smell prey under ice. They can smell a seal under the ice from two kilometres away.

Some birds also have an extraordinary sense of smell. A turkey vulture can smell a dead animal hidden under leaves as it flies one kilometre high over a forest.

Polar bear

Turkey vultures

Pit viper

Hidden senses

Some animals can sense the body heat of other animals. Snakes such as pit vipers have heat-sensitive pits on each side of their nostrils. These pits allow snakes to sense the body heat of animals that are nearby. They make a kind of heat picture similar to the way in which your eyes make a visual picture. As the snake moves closer, heat sensors inside its mouth tell it exactly where the prey is so the snake can strike and **paralyse** its prey.

Chapter 4:

Special body parts

Many animals have special body parts that they use like tools to help them get their food. Some animals have a long neck or a long tongue. Other animals have mouths, beaks, claws or hands to help them get food.

Think about ...

Think about some of the animals that live in your neighbourhood. What special body parts does each animal have to help it survive?

Giraffe

Chameleon

Aye-aye lemur

Hippopotamus

Long fingers

Some animals have an extra-long finger on each hand, which they use to catch insects and other animals to eat.

The aye-aye lemur has one finger that is longer than its other fingers on each hand. It uses this to catch grubs and insects under the bark and in holes in trees.

The striped possum of northern Australia also has one long finger on each hand that it uses in a similar way to the aye-aye lemur.

Chameleon

Aye-aye lemur

Find out more

The aye-aye lemur eats grubs and insects that it finds under bark and in holes in trees. Which one of its senses does it use to help it find food?

Long tongues

Some animals have incredibly long tongues, which they use to catch food.

A chameleon has a long, sticky tongue. When a chameleon senses an insect nearby, its tongue shoots out and wraps around the insect, pulling it back into the chameleon's mouth.

An anteater also has a very long tongue. An anteater eats ants and termites. It uses its powerful claws to rip open ant and termite nests. It pushes its long **snout** into the opening and traps the insects on its long, sticky tongue.

How long is that tongue?

- The giant anteater is found in Central and South America. It is about the size of a large dog. Its tongue is more than 60 centimetres long.
- A chameleon's tongue is longer than its body, from the tip of its nose to the end of its tail.

25

Birds and their beaks

Have you ever wondered why some birds have long thin beaks, while others have short hooked ones? It's all about food. A bird's beak or bill is ideally suited to finding the food that it eats in a particular place.

Birds use their beaks to gather food. Birds do not have teeth. Some birds use their beaks to crack open nuts; others use them to tear their food apart.

How birds use their beaks

Cracking
Type of beak
Hooked
Which birds?
Cockatoos and parrots use their strong hooked beaks to crack open hard nuts and seeds.

Chiseling
Type of beak
Thick
Which birds?
Woodpeckers have strong thick beaks to help them **chisel** into wood to gather grubs and beetles.

Grasping
Type of beak
Hooked
Which birds?
Penguins have hooked bills and spiny tongues to help them grasp slippery fish.

Prying
Type of beak
Long and pointed
Which birds?
Oystercatchers use their long, pointed bills to lever shells apart or crack them.

Beak or bill?

What is the difference between a beak and a bill?

There is no difference; they are the same thing.

Probing
Type of beak
Long and thin
Which birds?
Ibis use their long thin bills to probe the soft earth for worms.

Tearing
Type of beak
Hooked
Which birds?
Birds of prey have strong hooked bills that they use to tear their food apart.

Spearing
Type of beak
Dagger-like
Which birds?
Herons have a bill like a dagger that they use to spear fish.

Sifting
Type of beak
Spoon-shaped
Which birds?
Spoonbills have spoon-shaped bills that they use to sift tiny animals from shallow waters.

Sucking
Type of beak
Long and curved
Which birds?
Hummingbirds and honeyeaters have long curved bills to reach nectar deep inside flowers.

27

Chapter 5:

Using tools

Some animals use tools to help them get food and water. Some use sticks and twigs to poke into nests. Others use rocks to crack open nuts and eggs.

Using sticks as tools

Chimpanzees use twigs to catch termites. They remove any leaves to make the twig into a tool. They poke the twig into holes in a termite mound. As the chimp twists and vibrates the twig, the termites attack the twig and cling to it. The chimp then pulls the twig out and eats the termites.

Chimpanzees also poke sticks into the nests of honey bees to collect honey, which they lick from the stick.

Some birds also use twigs and sticks to get food in the same way as the chimpanzees of Africa. They use twigs and sticks, which they hold in their beaks, to force insect **larvae** out of their hiding places on tree trunks and branches. Once the insect larvae are out in the open, the birds eat them.

Did you know?
Chimpanzees use small leafy branches to help them get water. They chew the leaves to make them spongy and then put the branch in the water. The spongy leaves soak up the water. The chimpanzees then suck the water from the leaves.

Chimpanzees

Using twigs

The orange-winged sittella of Australia uses twigs to catch insects. It holds a twig in its beak and pokes the twig into holes that contain insect larvae in tree trunks. As the insect larvae are forced out of their hiding place, the bird holds the twig with its feet and eats the larvae with its beak.

Orange-winged sittella

29

Find out more

Gorillas, orangutans and dolphins can sometimes use tools. Find out how they do this.

Using stones and rocks as tools

Some birds use rocks and stones to get food. They throw rocks and stones at eggs with hard shells to break them open.

The Australian black-breasted buzzard eats emu eggs. Emu eggs have a very strong shell that the buzzard cannot break with its beak. The buzzard finds a stone, which it picks up in its beak and throws at the egg. It continues to throw the stone until the egg finally cracks open.

Buzzard

Glossary

adapted something or someone that has changed to suit its environment

chisel a long tool with a sharp cutting edge on the end

echolocation some animals make clicking sounds that bounce off hard objects like an echo, which tells the animal the location of the object

heat sensors organs that some snakes have near their jaws that help them sense heat

hind limbs the back legs of an animal that has more than one pair of legs

larvae the newly hatched wormlike form of many insects

mating ritual the actions that a pair of animals of the same species goes through before they produce their young

paralyse to make an animal unable to move

senses organs in an animal's body that it uses to obtain information about its environment

snout the long part of an animal's head that contains its nose and jaws

species a biological grouping of closely related living things

swim bladder a bag filled with gas that helps a fish stay at a certain depth in the water

vertebrae a series of small bones, with nerves running through them, that make up the backbone of an animal

Index

beaks 4, 22, 26–27, 29, 30
breeding grounds 13
claws 22, 25
diving 12, 15, 17
ears 4, 18
echolocation 16, 18, 31
eyes 4, 16, 17, 21
feathers 15
feet 15, 29
fingers 10, 24
fins 14
flippers 14–15
flying 4, 8, 12–13
hands 10, 22, 24
hearing 4, 16, 18, 19
heat sensors 16, 21, 31
jumping 8, 11

mouths 6, 21, 22, 25
necks 17, 22
noses 4, 6, 25
nostrils 21
running 4, 8, 9
seeing 13, 16, 17, 19
senses 4, 16–21, 25, 31
smell 6, 16, 20
snout 25, 31
sound 18–19
swim bladder 14, 31
swimming 4, 8, 14–15
taste 16, 20
tongues 4, 22, 25, 26
tools 4, 22, 28–29, 30
trunks 4, 6–7